Rub My Tummy and It's a Deal

An Andertoons Book of Business Cartoons
by Mark Anderson

Andertoons

Acknowledgments

Thanks to my family, loyal clients and customers,
Mike, Mark, Stephanie, Casey, Dave, Hilary, the guys
at Karma, and cartoon fans who laugh easily and often.

First published in the United States of America by Andertoons, LLC.

Visit us online at www.andertoons.com

Many of the cartoons in this books were first published in The American
Legion Magazine, Barron's, Brandweek, The Chronicle of Higher
Education, Commonweal, Forbes, Funny Times, Good Housekeeping,
Harvard Business Review, Psychiatry Weekly, Reader's Digest, The
Rotarian, The Saturday Evening Post, The Wall Street Journal, Woman's
World, USA Weekend, and on greeting cards by Allport Editions, Gallant
Greetings, and Papyrus.

Anderson, Mark
    Rub My Tummy and it's a Deal - An Andertoons Book of Business
    Cartoons by Mark Anderson
    1. Business--Caricatures and cartoons. 2. American wit and humor,
    Pictorial.

Library of Congress Control Number: 2008902740

ISBN-978-0-6151-9921-4

for Margie

Introduction

Mark is not a lucky guy. When I see a cartoon of Mark's – let's say, for instance, a guy in a meeting who asks, "I think I speak for all of us when I say what in God's name are you talking about?" – it's an event Mark lived through, for real, like the rest of us.

Before I met Mark, I knew him by his cartoons. And I liked what I saw. His cartoons showed a bumbling corporate world where business people

- try to use coupons in an acquisition;
- attempt to weaselword an employee firing, calling it a new exciting "exit-level position;"
- are happy to see satisfaction levels rising now that the complaint forms are eliminated.

Like me, Mark worked for a long while in a "real" job before becoming a full-time cartoonist. Like me, he now makes money from making fun of that same office world he used to work in.

I'm glad that he got out of cubicle life so he could produce all these cartoons for us to enjoy, but, like I said, it wasn't luck. It was hard work. In the beginning, he didn't have a drawing table. He would sit on the floor and put his paper on the coffee table and draw there, producing hundreds of cartoons, and getting many rejections in the beginning.

Mark built his own Web site, tweaking it and changing it; adding a blog, a huge Andertoon search function, and easy shopping for customers. Now, he's got a real drawing board – as well as a happy and healthy family.

And now here is his first Andertoon collection; a dinky fraction of his cartoony output. I'm glad to see Mark between these pages, rather than in some long, rambling business meeting.

Take it away, my inky brother!

- Mike Lynch

"I like you, Thompson. You're smart, a hard
worker, and you're full of potassium."

"Of course, this is a worst case scenario."

"What's that boy?! A paradigm shift?!"

"Do me a favor and call Tom. It looks like
Jerry is on to something."

"Tell them we're drowning in maroon ink. It sounds better."

"And how long were you in
hunting/gathering?"

"Motivational listener."

"He's right, when you look at it that way,
it's not so bad!"

"Who's the new guy?"

"You the temp?"

"I'm sorry, Tom, we're downsizing and, well, you're the tallest."

"We find it helps our less motivated
employees."

"For another ten bucks I can also read your palm pilot."

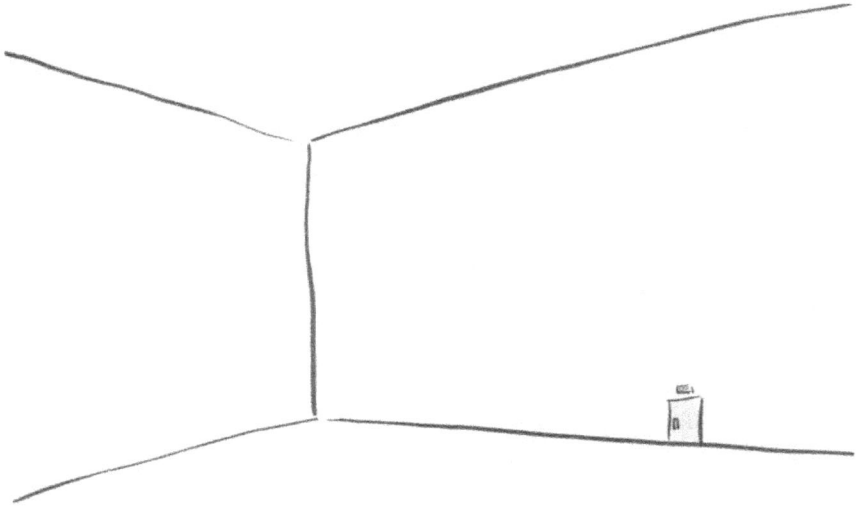

"What do you say we start insourcing again."

"I'd say take it up with management, but
that's me, so just ignore it."

"We're playing teleconference."

Sara, have sales do that thing where profits go up."

"Yes, well, root of evil though it may be, you
still have to pay the invoice."

"I thought it sounded better than 'Out of Business'."

"It's times like these we really need to roll up our sleeves, rally together and find ourselves a scapegoat."

"I don't get it. Everytime I try to take inventory, I nod off!"

"I think I have an idea."

"We find our younger employees respond better to 'try to beat your high score,' than 'we need to increase profits.'"

"There's a lot of fine print; let me get my reading coals."

"Technically I work for money like everyone else, but, yes, most of it does go for peanuts."

"It's not just a raise in my allowance, it's also
a boost for consumer confidence!"

"I was on the fast track, now I'm just kinda off-roading."

"Maybe it's time we kept a little
for ourselves."

"Let's see... Inside sales, VP of sales....
Ooh! King of the jungle! Very nice!"

"You work hard, Tim, but I'm worried you're not playing hard enough."

"I think I found the problem with your spreadsheet -- it's a sudoku."

"I'm not as worried about the glass ceiling as
I am about the glass walls and floor."

"We're really more of a department."

ANDERSON & SONS

CREATING AN AWKWARD WORKPLACE THROUGH NEPOTISM SINCE 1963

"We're still not sure what happened here, but I think we can all agree that we're glad it's over."

"I don't have any answers. I'm a non-prophet."

IN CASE OF PAPER JAM BREAK GLASS

ANDERSON

"Sales are through the roof!"

"How goes the merger?"

"Looks like it'll run around $400. Wall Street's
estimates, however, are not so rosy."

"Tell you what, rub my tummy and it's
a deal."

"Industry insiders are cautiously optimistic.
Industry outsiders don't much care."

"No, it's fine, I've just never seen coupons
used in an acquisition."

"It appears to be some sort of pyramid
scheme."

"Not only is it lonely at the top, but I'm afraid of heights."

"I'm disappointed; if anyone should have
seen the red flags, it's you."

"How do I love thee? I had my people put
some numbers together."

"No, I distinctly remember sending you to a seminar."

"I think I speak for all of us when I say what in God's name are you talking about?"

"Finally, to help those of us counting carbs, we've moved to bar graphs instead of pie charts."

MANAGE A TROIS

"Anderson, don't forget, I need that bratwurst on my desk by three!"

"You know, it was a great fall!"

"Technically, we're not firing you. We're just moving you into an exit level position."

"I was making money hand over fist. Then I got carpal tunnel."

"I'm not content, people. I'm not content
at all."

"It's really more of a lateral move, which is great for me!"

"Oh, that. OSHA stopped by the other day..."

"And this is Tom, our chief bling officer."

"Due to recent economic conditions, picture worth has dropped to an all time low of 842 words."

"Granted, there were no blenders in the stone age, so technically that was our all time low, but this is still pretty bad."

"I'd like to meet you halfway, but I'm terrible with fractions."

"Don't you think this internal audit's gone too far?"

"I suppose technically all of our offices are branch offices."

"What, you didn't hear about the merger?"

"This is Bert. He's going to help us clear out
our dead wood."

"'Of course, these are just ballpark numbers."

"No, the end of November is bad for me."

"Business has really gone south, so we're
moving the company to Texas."

"The new font is great, but I still don't like
the look of these numbers."

"What happens to the stock when I do this?"

"So, where do you see yourself in ten minutes?"

"I love your business model!"

"We prefer to call it micro-management."

"Oh, great..."

"How much to get promotion written all over me?"

"No, that's fine. Morale is supposed
to be bad."

"Listen, we're dominating honey, maybe it's time we diversify into jelly."

"Santa's outsourcing."

"You gotta admit, it's a catchy jingle."

"Arbitrators in the Alaskan Ice strike talks have recommended a seven day warming up period."

ANDERSON

"Not to be argumentative, but go to hell, Ernie."

"I'd love to, but I've got the Muffet thing this morning, and water spouts all afternoon."

"So, as you can see, customer satisfaction is up considerably since phasing out the complaint forms."

"It's never fun firing anyone, Tim. So, to liven things up, here's Donald Trump."

REGULAR

DECAF

TROUBLE

ANDERSON

"We desperately need to hire someone, but
everyone is declining to be interviewed."

"Our parent company is pleased with our progress, but they want to know why we never call."

"This one's a real no-brainer. That's why I asked for you specifically."

"We'd like to give you this empty cardboard box as our way of saying we'd like you out by three."

"No, I'm a full-time employee, I just work part-time."

"While we have only a small piece of the pie,
we own the whipped cream."

"Things went from bad to worse, but we're hopeful now that we're doing badly again."

"So, it says here on your resume that you're a giraffe."

"OK, now that we all agree, let's all go back
to our desks and discuss why this
won't work."

www.ingramcontent.com/pod-product-compliance
Lightning Source LLC
Chambersburg PA
CBHW022306060426
42446CB00007BA/729